LITTLE BOOK
OF GRATITUDE

Jacqueline Kademian

Positive Soul LLC

DEDICATION

This book is dedicated to my Positive Soul community, family, friends, boyfriend and loved ones. . I am so grateful for all of you and am honored to have you on this journey. Gratitude will take each of us far. Know that I am grateful for all of you and will continue to do my best so inspire you.

CONTENTS

ACKNOWLEDGMENTS

I want to thank the beautiful souls who have helped me write this book. To my loved ones and clients', thank you!

INTRODUCTION

Welcome!

Welcome to the Little Book Of Gratitude! I am so excited that you've decided to purchase this journal and transform your life. Thank you for being here and making the time to be grateful.

This journal is so meaningful for so many reasons. For starters, it's a gratitude journal unlike any of those on the market. I'm a journal lover, so you know I had to make something different than what was out there.

Instead of using the same gratitude prompts, I decided to make this experience even more transformative and beneficial for you. What you find inside this journal is unique, transformative and life changing.

This journal is extremely powerful and life changing because it hones in on one of the most powerful energies of the universe, gratitude. I know you've heard of gratitude a million times on your self development journey, but why is it so important?

To put it simply, gratitude is a practice that has the potential to change your life. Being grateful and appreciative for what you have opens up the door for more amazing things to come in.

When you are grateful for the present moment, you're able to enjoy your life and actually *live,* not just exist. Gratitude is also one of the most powerful vibrations of the Universe, as being grateful improves your quality of life.

I know you know all of this, because let's face

it, you are brilliant!

There are not enough words to explain why gratitude is important. Not only does it improve your quality of life, it improves your physical health and mental health. Gratitude impacts the way you act in relationships. It improves your interactions with others. It improves your interactions with yourself. It has the power to transform all aspects of your life.

Now with such an amazing transformation, you'd think that practicing gratitude would be difficult. Guess what? It's not at all.

Gratitude journals and practices seem so simple and basic, yet the results are extraordinary. Doing a basic gratitude practice each day can have a host of benefits. It doesn't have to be complicated to have a big impact, remember that.

In this journal, you'll find a fresh new spin on gratitude. I wanted to focus the entire journal on gratitude and appreciation, because I know just how gratitude can change your life.

Each day, you will be asked to take an aspect of your life and express your gratitude. The questions are thought provoking, self reflective and transformative. Like my other journal, Soul Therapy, this journal is meant to take you on a journey of self discovery and personal development. You'll find that when you are done with this little book, you're going to be a different person.

How It Works

This journal is a gratitude practice in action.
Each day, you will be asked to reflect upon an
aspect of your life that you are grateful for.
It's easy, simple and perfect for a daily
practice.

The journal is an open space for you to be
creative. Write down anything that comes to

your mind as you read the prompt. It's free-flowing and the open space is for you to be as creative as possible.

Be as consistent with this journal as much as possible. You may miss a day or not feel like doing it on some days, but the more consistent you can be, the better! You are forming an extremely positive habit with this journal, so be as consistent as you can be.

For best results, pick a time of day that you can complete your journal entry. It's also recommended to do only one journal prompt per day.

The prompts are simple and they shouldn't take more than 5-10 minutes.

Sometimes, you may feel stuck about certain topics. In those moments, let your mind wander and then write what comes to mind. Even in negative situations, there is always something we can be grateful for.

There are dates at the top of each prompt so you keep track. This way, you can start the journal at any point of the year.

Lastly, have fun with this! Be creative. Be present. This journal will evoke different feelings in you. Some prompts may allow you to look at yourself more deeply. Be present as you complete this journal, as it has the power to change your life.

I'm so grateful for you being here. Let's begin.

Date _____

I am so grateful and happy now that the
Universe is helping me manifest...

Date _____

What experience are you thankful to that you had, that has taught you something important? Reflect upon what you are grateful for about that experience.

Date _____

Name 10 things you are grateful for about
your body.

Date _____

What choices have you made in the last year that you'd thank yourself for making?

Date _____

Name 5 things in your home that you are grateful for. Reflect upon what each belonging does for you.

Date _____

Write about a family member that you're grateful for. What does this person mean to you?

Date _____

Being grateful in advance of your goals
manifesting is a powerful practice. Write
about all of the goals you are grateful for that
you will manifest in the next year.

Date _____

If you are in a relationship, name 10 things you are grateful for about your partner. If you are not currently in a relationship, name 10 things you will be grateful for about your future partner *(manifestation in process)*.

Date _____

What holidays are you grateful for and why?
What makes them special?

Date _____

Name 10 things you are grateful for about your family.

Date _____

Write about a happy memory you are thankful
for.

Date _____

What's a possession that makes your life easier?

Date _____

What's something that you bought recently that you're grateful for?

Date _____

I am grateful for these relationships that did not work out…

Date _____

What are you the most grateful for about the current time you live in?

Date _____

I am grateful for my ability to…

Date _____

Pick someone in your life to write a special letter to below. Write about what you are most grateful about them.

Date _____

Name 10 things you are grateful for about
your current home.

Date _____

What do you love about your daily schedule?

Date _____

What skills or abilities are you grateful to have?

Date _____

How is where you are in life today different than a year ago, and what positive changes are you grateful for?

Date _____

What elements of nature are you thankful for and why?

Date _____

Write about your favorite musician/band and what you are grateful for about their music.

Date _____

Who has helped you become the person you are today, and what would you thank them for?

Date _____

What do you like about your job?

Date _____

What foods or meals are you most grateful for to eat?

Date _____

I am grateful about this recent opportunity…

Date _____

Write about a few friends you are grateful for and why. Describe what each friend means to you.

Date _____

I am grateful for these gifts I have received…

Date _____

What small thing happened today that you are grateful for?

Date _____

Which of your personality traits are you
grateful for?

Date _____

I am grateful for this person who always puts me in a good mood…

Date _____

Describe a family tradition you are most grateful for. Reflect upon the tradition and what it means to you.

Date _____

What experience are you thankful to that you had, that has taught you something important?

Date _____

What are you grateful for about your health?

Date _____

In contrast to one of my hardest days, I am grateful for today because. . .

Date _____

What are you the most grateful for about the current time you live in?

Date _____

I am grateful for these goals I have
achieved…

Date _____

Name 10 things you are grateful for about
your personality.

Date _____

How has gratitude changed your life? What positive changes have you noticed?

Date _____

What's something that you're looking forward to?

Date _____

Write about a teacher or mentor that you're grateful for.

Date _____

What's a simple pleasure that makes you happy?

Date _____

What positive qualities have you picked up
from your parents that you are grateful for?

Date _____

Can you think of any non-physical gifts
you've received recently—someone's time,
attention, understanding, or support, that
made you feel extremely grateful?

Date _____

What's something that you grateful to have today that you didn't have a year ago?

Date _____

I am grateful for these books I have read…

Date _____

What are you grateful for about your sense of taste?

Date _____

What is your least favorite kind of weather?
Think of 3 things about it to be grateful for.

Date _____

One of the best things about being married/
single/in a relationship is. . .

Date _____

What's a possession that makes your life easier? Why are you grateful for it?

Date _____

Open your phone or photo album and find a photo that you like. Why are you grateful for this photo?

Date _____

Name 10 things you are grateful for about the city you were born in.

Date _____

What have you been given as a present that you're grateful for? Reflect upon the best gifts you've ever received.

Date _____

What luxury are you lucky to have access to?

Date _____

What artist, author, or musician are you grateful for?

Date _____

What is something unique about your family
that you're grateful for?

Date _____

Name 10 things you are grateful for about
your appearance.

Date _____

What public services or organizations are you grateful for?

Date _____

I appreciate the following things about my job/work. . .

Date _____

What's one kind or thoughtful thing someone did for you recently?

Date _____

I am grateful for these simple pleasures I can enjoy daily…

Date _____

Who is someone you have never met that you are grateful for?

Date _____

What did you accomplish today?

Date _____

What mistake or failure are you grateful for?
What did it teach you?

Date _____

What choices have you made in the last five years that you'd thank yourself for making?

Date _____

Name 20 things you are grateful about
yourself. Write about anything that comes to
mind.

Date _____

What are you grateful for about nature?

Date _____

How do your spiritual beliefs or practices
fulfill your life?

Date _____

I am grateful for these people who gave me an opportunity...

Date _____

Who is someone you have a hard time getting along with? Think of at least 3 positive qualities about that person you can be thankful for.

Date _____

Name 10 things you are grateful for about
your extended family.

Date _____

I'm grateful for these technological gadgets
that make my life easier…

Date _____

Write about 3 special opportunities you have had in your life that you have been grateful for.

Date _____

I am grateful for an amazing opportunity I
have been given to…

Date _____

What skills or abilities do you have that
you're grateful for?

Date _____

What time of year are you most grateful for
and why?

Date _____

What's something that has inspired or touched you recently?

Date _____

Look around the room and write about
everything you see that you're thankful for.

Date _____

I am grateful for this special place I can go for peace and quiet…

Date _____

What positive qualities have you picked up from your friends that you are grateful for?

Date _____

Write about your five senses and what you are grateful for about each one.

Date _____

Name 10 things you are grateful for about
your current job/business.

Date _____

Who have you enjoyed being around recently, and why? What are you grateful for about this person?

Date _____

What are you grateful for about your intuition?

Date _____

What TV shows/movies are you most grateful
for? How do they improve your life?

Date _____

Name 10 things you are grateful for about
your parents.

Date _____

What are a few things you are grateful for
about mornings?

Date _____

One of your most worthwhile purchases that you can't live without has been. . .

Date _____

If all of your dreams came true a year from now, what would you be grateful for happening?

Date _____

What moment this week are you most grateful for?

Date _____

I am grateful to these animals…

Date _____

How can you be grateful for a perceived weakness that you have?

Date _____

Write about a certain situation or experience
that ended up being "a blessing in disguise".
What are you grateful for about that
experience?

Date _____

I wouldn't be where I am today without this person's help and support. . .

Date _____

What's something you witnessed recently that reminded you that life is good? Write about that experience and what it taught you.

Date _____

What is something enjoyable you get to
experience every day that you possibly take
for granted?

Date _____

What are you grateful for that you have learned today, that you didn't know a few years ago?

Date _____

Name 10 things you are grateful for about the generation you were born in.

Date _____

What are 5 things your arms or legs allow you to do?

Date _____

How does electricity simplify and improve your life? Express your gratitude.

Date _____

Write a list of positive things that have happened to you over the past week and why you are grateful for them.

Date _____

What is working in your life? How thankful
are you that it is?

Date _____

I am grateful for these family members…

Date _____

What positive changes are you grateful for having made in your life?

Date _____

Write about your favorite emotions and why you are grateful to be able to feel them.

Date _____

What invention are you truly grateful for having access to?

Date _____

Name 10 things you are grateful for about your friends.

Date _____

What are you thankful for not having?

Date _____

What are 3 good decisions you've made this year, that has improved your life?

Date _____

Write a letter to someone expressing your thanks to them.

Date _____

Today, I can show my gratitude to others and myself by…

Date _____

Name 10 possessions of yours you are grateful for having.

Date _____

Describe a relationship that helped shape you into the person you are today. What are you grateful for about this relationship?

Date _____

What body part or organ are you most grateful for today?

Date _____

Write about any musician, author, artist, entertainer you are grateful for and what they mean to you.

Date _____

Describe the sense that you are most grateful for today.

Date _____

List 10 items that you take for granted, which might not be available to others in other parts of the world (example; clean water, electricity, food)

Date _____

I am grateful for these experience I have had...

Date _____

What is one aspect about your health that you're more grateful for today than you were a year ago?

Date _____

What are you grateful for about your childhood?

Date _____

What is one thing you are thankful you can enjoy each day?

Date _____

What are you grateful for about your sense of
smell?

Date _____

What is your favorite quote or piece of advice
that you are grateful for?

Date _____

What is your favorite season and why are you grateful for it?

Date _____

I am grateful for these holidays that I can enjoy…

Date _____

If someone was looking into your life from the outside, what would they say you should be grateful for in your life?

Date _____

What is something that comes easily to you, but is challenging for others?

Date _____

What freedoms are you most grateful for?

Date _____

Which self care activities do you enjoy, which you are grateful you get to do?

Date _____

What is one something you've learned this week that you're grateful for?

Date _____

List 10 ways you can share your gratitude and thanks with others in the next 24 hours.

Date _____

Write about places in your city you are
grateful for, that you can go to and enjoy.

Date _____

I am grateful for these things I am good at…

Date _____

What body part or organ are you most
grateful for today? Share your appreciation.

Date _____

What are a few aspects of modern technology that you are grateful for?

Date _____

Are you a morning or night person? What are you the most grateful for about this part of the day?

Date _____

Name 10 qualities about yourself that others have told you they are grateful for.

Date _____

Write a letter to someone who has impacted
your life in the past month. Describe why you
are thankful for this person.

Date _____

Write about your favorite part about every season and why you are grateful for it.

Date _____

I am grateful for these life lessons I have
learned…

Date _____

What are you grateful for about your sense of hearing?

Date _____

List a few qualities you dislike about yourself,
then list something you are grateful for about
each quality.

Date _____

Where was your favorite trip you have ever taken? Write about your trip and what you were grateful for about it.

Date _____

Reflect about the last time you laughed really hard and write how that experience made you feel.

Date _____

Write about something in your life that you
love doing for fun, and why you are grateful
you are able to do this.

Date _____

Write about why you are grateful for the place
you grew up in.

Date _____

What are you grateful for about your hands and what they allow you to do?

Date _____

Think back to a year ago, and write down the differences in your life then to now, and why you are grateful for these changes

Date _____

List 10 skills you are grateful you have, that most people don't possess.

Date _____

Write down how you can show gratitude
towards other people in your life.

Date _____

What is one aspect about your health that
you're more grateful for today than you were
a year ago?

Date _____

What is your least favorite emotion to feel?
Name how this emotion can teach you
something, and how you can be grateful for it.

Date _____

What are you grateful for about getting older?

Date _____

Write about how appreciative you are to have the time to write about gratitude in this journal.

Date _____

What are you the most grateful for about your life and why?

Date _____

Describe the gratitude you feel for your eyes and being able to read the words on this page.

Date _____

Write about 5 things you are grateful for that happened today.

Date _____

What am I grateful for that I learned in school?

Date _____

Who are your role models and why are you grateful for them?

Date _____

What new relationship in your life are you grateful for?

Date _____

Look around the room you are in and write about everything you see that you are grateful for.

Date _____

I am grateful to these things I get to hear…

Date _____

What are you grateful for about your sense of touch?

Date _____

Think about a possession that you own and write about the gratitude you feel for what it allows you to do.

Date _____

Who is someone you have never met that you are grateful for?

Date _____

I am grateful for those people in my
community that…

Date _____

Express gratitude for the way you get around your city.

Date _____

Think about each of your body parts and write one thing you are grateful for about each one.

Date _____

I am grateful for these people who never gave up on me…

Date _____

Reflect upon how writing about gratitude for these past 6 months has been like for you. What have you learned about yourself?

Date _____

Some of the best things about my job/
business that I am grateful for are…

Date _____

What moment this week are you most grateful for?

Date _____

Think back to 3 months ago. What are you thankful for that has changed over the past few months?

Date _____

I am so grateful and happy now that the
Universe is helping me manifest…

Date _____

I am so grateful to this teacher/mentor who taught me that…

Date _____

What was the last conversation you had that made you more grateful for that relationship?

Date _____

What choices have you made in the last year that you'd thank yourself for making?

Date _____

What are you more grateful for today, that
you weren't as grateful for a year ago?

Date _____

How has gratitude changed your life and shaped who you are today?

Date _____

Let's end this journal on a love note. Write about everything you are grateful and appreciative for in your life. Make sure to write about the most important person in your life, you.

ABOUT THE AUTHOR

Jacqueline Kademian is a Licensed Marriage & Family Therapist and Coach. She is the creator of the personal development brand, Positive Soul. She uses spirituality and psychology techniques to help others create massive changes in their lives. She is able to provide healing and transformation by helping her clients' find their power and greatness.

If you'd like to find out more about Jacqueline and the other products she offers, visit her on her website, https://positivesoul.net. You can also find her on Instagram, @positive___soul, where she posts inspirational content.

You can also view her other books, Soul Therapy & You Are That Girl on Amazon.

Manufactured by Amazon.ca
Bolton, ON